What Is F

Written by Rozanne Lanczak Williams
Created by Sue Lewis
Illustrated by Patty Briles

Creative Teaching Press

What Is Funny?
© 2002 Creative Teaching Press, Inc.
Written by Rozanne Lanczak Williams
Illustrated by Patty Briles
Project Manager: Sue Lewis
Project Director: Carolea Williams

Published in the United States of America by:
Creative Teaching Press, Inc.
P.O. Box 2723
Huntington Beach, CA 92647-0723

All rights reserved. No part of this book may be reproduced in any form without the written permission of Creative Teaching Press, Inc.

CTP 3219

What is funny? A funny face.

A fast, funny fox.

A fat, funny fish.

A funny little box.

Five funny fingers.

Four funny feet.

Five funny farmers.

And four funny sheep!

Create your own book!

Have a fun time writing and illustrating your own funny book. Use words beginning with *f* and other words you know.

Words in *What Is Funny?*

Initial Consonant: *f*
funny
face
fast
fox
fat
fish
five
fingers
four
feet
farmers

High-Frequency Words
what
is
a
and

Other
box
sheep
little